THIS BOOK IS F

. . . .

THE WORLD'S MOST CHARMING/
OFFENSIVE/ KISSABLE/PATHETIC/
FOUL/UGLY/BEAUTIFUL/TAUREAN

WITH KIND REGARDS/DROP DEAD/
LOVE AND KISSES. . . . .

P.S. PLEASE TAKE NOTE OF PAGE(S)

. . . .

Ian Heath's Taurus Book

ISBN 1-905134-04-5

Published by Ian Heath Books
9 Adam Street
The Strand
London WC2N 6AA
www.ianheathart.com

/anheath's

TAURUS
BOOK

TAURUS

APRIL 21 – MAY 20

SECOND SIGN OF THE ZODIAC
SYMBOL : THE BULL
RULING PLANET : VENUS
COLOURS : DEEP ROSE, DEEP BLUE
GEMS : TURQUOISE, SAPPHIRE
NUMBER : SIX
DAY : FRIDAY
METAL : COPPER
FLOWER : FORGET-ME-NOT

.........IS INDUSTRIOUS............

.....A STICKLER FOR DETAIL........

...FRIENDLY TO CO-WORKERS.....

.........NEVER SHOUTS..........

.... REMAINS COOL IN A CRISIS.....

.... IS DECISIVE..............

.... CREATIVE ....

....CAN GET IN A RUT...........

.......ARRIVES EARLY...............

...... AND STAYS LATE.

.........AN OPERA SINGER..........

.... PLUMBER....................

............JOCKEY...................

.... CHIROPODIST.............

.... TOWN CRIER ....

The TAUREAN at home............

.....ENJOYS ROMANTIC MUSIC........

.... WALLPAPERING ....

.... IS INTO D.I.Y. ....

.... KEEPS ANIMALS ....

.......NEEDS SECURITY...........

...... ADORES GARDENING ....

. . . . .LIKES TO RELAX . . . .

.... IS SUPPORTIVE...........

.... COLLECTS OBJETS D'ART.........

.....AND IS HOUSE-PROUD.

.... SMART CLOTHES ....

............FISHING...................

.... SKIING...................

..... LEARNING LANGUAGES ....

.... CAMPING ....

.... AND BOILED EGGS.

The TAUREAN
dislikes.................

...... WASHING -UP................

.... DANDRUFF...............

......CRYSTALLIZED FRUIT.........

.... DECEITFULNESS..............

.... RABID DOGS...............

.... AND BEING ILL.

The TAUREAN in love..............

.... IS JEALOUS ....

.... SINCERE ....

. . . . STUBBORN . . . .

.... CALCULATING ....

.... FAITHFUL ....

.... DEMANDING ....

.... VERY CHOOSY...............

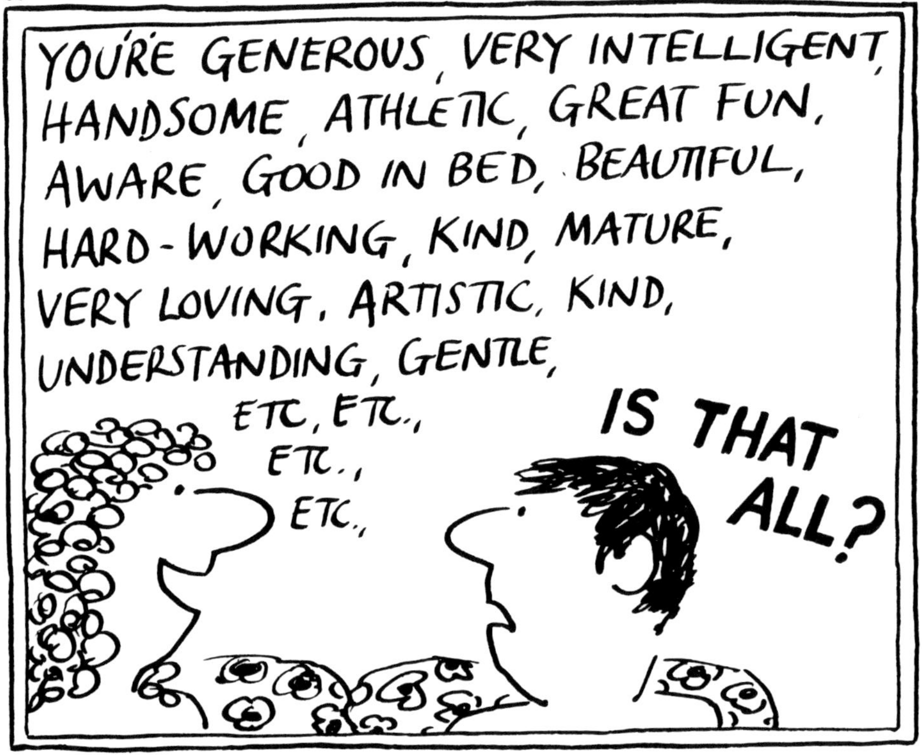

...ENJOYS BEING FLATTERED.......

...AND LIKES THE LIGHTS OUT.

TAUREAN AND PARTNER

HEART RATINGS

♥♥♥♥♥ WOWEE!!

♥♥♥♥ GREAT, BUT NOT 'IT'

♥♥♥ O.K. — COULD BE FUN

♥♥ FORGET IT

♥ WALK QUICKLY THE OTHER WAY

VIRGO CAPRICORN

GEMINI CANCER PISCES
ARIES

AQUARIUS LEO TAURUS

SCORPIO

LIBRA SAGITTARIUS